A Puppy's Perspective
101 Puppy Training Tips You Need to Know

KIM PACIOTTI
with Christina Borders

Training Canines, LLC
302 Valley Stream Road
Statesville, NC 28677
www.trainingcanines.com

Book Layout © 2017 BookDesignTemplates.com

A Puppy's Perspective/ Kim Paciotti, CPDT-KA — 1st ed.
ISBN 978-0-692-04301-1

This book is dedicated to my inspiration, my girl Sabre, for giving me the reason to take the leap to becoming a dog trainer. Instead of trying to "fix" her, as many trainers said would never happen, I learned she had an individual personality that needed help understanding our world. I made a promise to her the day she crossed the rainbow bridge that I would do all I could to never let another puppy be misunderstood.

Acknowledgments

To my husband, David, thank you doesn't seem enough. You sacrificed and worked so hard for our family, yet you gave me the opportunity to pursue a long-desired dream of working with dogs. To this day you are the rock that holds it all together. I could never do this without you. I love you more than words can say.

To my kids, I thank you for all your understanding as schedules have been based around "we can't, what about the dogs" and what the puppies needed. I could not be prouder of, or more thankful for, both of you. Even though you are grown adults, the best part of the day is when I get to talk with you. I love you so much!

To my parents, I hope that I have made you proud. I thank you for your shoulders I cried on, your advice as I shared my struggles, your hugs as I shared my happiness, but most of all for caring enough to listen. I love you.

And to Christina, you are an amazing woman and the inspiration to write this book! You have been in this with me the last few years, in the good and bad. Days filled with puppies not feeling well, to days of pure joy when they understood what we were teaching. According to my daughter, you are a saint for even being able to work with me! I am forever grateful to you, as you are much more than a coworker—you are a forever friend.

CONTENTS

INTRODUCTION

These days it seems anyone can call themselves an expert on a subject or in a field of study. In our super-connected society, information is literally a click, tap, or Google search away. Quick fixes, miracle gadgets, and self-described 'professionals' abound, touting the answers and solutions many desperately need. But little relies on firsthand research and experience. What we tend to find are traditional methods and ideas that, while they may be effective, can be confusing and don't really 'fit' into our modern lives.

Dog training is no exception. Several years ago, and all of a sudden, my husband and I were facing behavior issues with our dog that began at the loss of another pet. Sabre, our ten-month-old English Mastiff, turned into Dr. Jekyll and Mr. Hyde. One minute she loved you, and the next she wanted to chomp your hand off. We looked for answers and interviewed many trainers. What we found was frustration. Everyone said something different. We even had one trainer say he was coming in a bite suit and it wouldn't be pretty. Well, he lasted all of one visit as Sabre wasn't having him in her house! Needless to say, I had to help her, and I had to learn why our adorable puppy suddenly changed.

Research began. I studied all I could, but it just made me more confused. There had to be a solution. To top off my frustrations with Sabre, it was 2008 and the economy was not in a great place. My career over the previous twenty-plus years had been as a professional chef. From owning and operating an event company, a bakery, and working at a local university, it was now time to follow the deep-rooted passion I had of working with dogs. Sabre gave me the reason to take the plunge, as I wanted so desperately to help her, and with what I learned I was finally able to make a difference in Sabre's life.

I learned that dog training was too generalized. I found that ironic, as dogs don't generalize well; however, many training programs were generalizing their training. You either had a good dog, a dominant dog, or an aggressive dog. There wasn't any consistent information on dogs that fell between these categories. Sabre didn't fit any of those stereotypes, so I was left still searching. I became a certified dog trainer through the Certificate Council for Professional Dog Trainers (CCPDT), and Training Canines LLC was born.

As part of my quest for answers, I explored many aspects of dog training, one of which was working with shelter and rescue dogs. To my surprise, many dogs that are surrendered are eight to nine months of age and many are the breed deemed most popular by the American Kennel Club (AKC): the Labrador Retriever. I would hear common complaints, and it seemed to me that many of the problems would have been easily avoided if the owners had just done a little more training when the puppies were young. My focus then began to concentrate on puppies. How they learn, what they learn, and what we could do to avoid or change temperament problems that were surfacing at the eight- to nine-month mark, which was around the same age Sabre's issues showed up. I wondered whether her problems really began due to grief at the death of our other dog or whether it was a disconnect from puppyhood.

The only way to get true answers was to start with the puppies as early as possible. We began to work with breeders who would let us bring the mother and puppies to our facility when the puppies were ten days old. We studied litter after litter, puppy after puppy, and the Empowered Puppy Program was born. Since that time, we have raised and placed hundreds of puppies that have proven early puppy development is the key to happy, healthy puppies and adult dogs.

With every litter we continue to marvel at how smart puppies are. What they can be taught is absolutely amazing. With this book we want to share with you some of our top tips that will truly make a difference in your and your puppy's lives.

TEMPERAMENT

Empowered Puppy Bite #106

The Scent

You can ease the transition of your puppy coming to your home by introducing your scent to them before they arrive. About a week or so before you pick them up, talk to your breeder about giving the puppy a towel or T-shirt with the scent of the people in your household on it. This will expose the puppy to your scent and they will be more likely to feel more comfortable with you when you pick them up. If you are able to give the breeder a small blanket or towel at the same time, the breeder can get the scent of the litter and the puppy's mom on it, which will comfort the puppy and help reduce anxiety.

Self-Esteem

Your dog has self-esteem, and it is your job to build it up. Let them know that you are proud of them. We have Cosmos, who gets so happy when he shows us he ate his food. We make a huge deal out of telling him he is such a good boy and we are so happy. He will actually prance around and act like "look at me!" It is so great to see that he's a confident dog because that spills over into other areas of training. Building self-esteem helps when teaching a nervous dog, because you can motivate him. Seeing happiness come over a dog is just the best thing.

Empowered Puppy Bite #91

Sudden Sounds

You want to get your puppy used to sudden sounds, and the easiest way to do this is by including it in your training. Simply have someone start yelling, and coach your puppy through it. Talk to them and reassure them that they don't have to worry, it is just someone yelling. Don't stop talking to your puppy and make sure your tone is very calm and monotone. The puppy will see that you are not scared, and they will learn they don't have to be scared, either.

11

Just Have Fun

One thing we want to remind you of as a new puppy or dog owner is to have fun. Don't be too serious if you make a mistake when training. Dogs are very forgiving. Love on them and hug them and just do the very best you can for them. They will appreciate you going with the flow and sometimes being a little silly, as it takes the pressure off them.

Empowered Puppy Bite #60

Naming People & Places

You can teach your puppy the names of the different rooms in your home. You can also teach names of family and friends. For example, if you want to teach the name of a person, you say the name of the puppy, and go to "the name" of the person. That person then immediately calls the puppy with the "here" command. This quickly teaches the puppy the name of the person.

Choosing a Name

It is time to name your new puppy and you are considering a bunch of options. We have found it beneficial to give the puppy a two-syllable name. When you say the name, it naturally comes out like you are singing. Pitch changes in our voice make the puppies take more notice of what we are saying. A name with two or more syllables fulfills this tone for our puppies and actually helps them pay closer attention to us.

Empowered Puppy Bite #41

Capturing Behaviors

It is very simple to strengthen good behaviors in your puppy. If you see them lying down being calm and quiet, walk up to them and tell them they're doing a great job. Reward them for giving you the behavior without having to be asked for it. Once you start doing that repetitively, you'll find that they offer that behavior much more quickly and reliably.

Capture Their Interest

When you are training your puppy, which really is all the time, you want to be interesting, not boring. If your puppy is very distracted and keeps leaving you or is not giving you their focus, you need to become interesting! Say or do silly things, talk in high-pitched tones, put some extra movement in your actions. Anything to get their attention so they realize what a fun person you are!

Empowered Puppy Bite #55

Trust is Earned

No matter how much you love your puppy or your dog, always remember that trust is earned and not automatically given. You have to build that relationship every day and in every interaction with them.

Do Not Overstimulate

People sometimes think they should tire their puppy out prior to bedtime by playing hard or going for a long walk. But as can happen with children, that tactic often has the opposite effect and makes the puppy become more awake. It is much easier to teach them to be calm and relaxed prior to going to bed, as then everyone will have a much more restful night.

Empowered Puppy Bite #96

Rotate Toys

When you first get your puppy you may well go out and buy a bunch of toys. Sometimes friends will send over a care package with something for the new arrival. But don't give them too many toys at one time or they will not learn how to play with them. Take a few and teach them how to interact with the toy. Add new toys and take away ones you have used for a while. Reintroduce those toys at a later date. Your puppy will think he is constantly getting something new and exciting.

Proactive not Reactive

Puppies are curious and they get into everything. They don't know that the funny-looking thing on the wall is an electrical socket. They don't know that is a sock and they shouldn't eat it. Puppies do not come preprogrammed to know that they shouldn't pee on the floor. Set your puppy up for success by puppy proofing your home. Get down on your hands and knees and look at things from their perspective. Remember that they are used to checking things out with their mouth, and usually everything goes in there first. You don't want it to go in and only come out by taking a trip to the vet!

Empowered Puppy Bite #29

Routines

Puppies and dogs thrive on us being predictable. Sometimes they know what we are going to do better than we ourselves know. The word to remember is *routine*. Your puppy must learn routine first, then you can teach them to go with the flow. Keeping a routine builds confidence so they think they can take on the world. Once they have this confidence, you can slowly introduce new ways and new things. By doing this, you shape a puppy into a very well-rounded dog.

Ignoring Novelties

Remember, when you're training (which is all the time), your puppy will have a hard time ignoring novelties. They will be seeing, hearing, smelling, and feeling things they have never experienced before. Allow them time to process on their own. Once they do, they will learn which distractions to block out.

Empowered Puppy Bite #94

Body Parts

A great way to teach your puppy about their body and get them used to being handled is to teach them the names of their body parts. We start this with our puppies when they are four to five weeks old. We hold the puppy, place a paw in our hand, give it an ever-so-slight squeeze and say, "right paw." We then do the left paw, the chin, the belly, the tail, the feet, and so on. We do it five times consecutively twice a day for about a week. Then we can ask them to put their belly on the ground and they lie down, or to put their bum on the ground and they sit. Naming the body parts encourages their learning and interaction with us.

Calming a Puppy

You can quickly help your puppy calm down by simply placing your open palm very gently at the top of the base of the tail. Hold it there for fifteen to twenty seconds. This stimulates nerve endings in the skin and sends soothing and calming messages back to the brain. It will help the puppy regain composure.

Empowered Puppy Bite #50

You Need to Explain

Walking your puppy is a great time to practice what we call "name and explain." You simply tell your puppy what they see or what they are sniffing, whether it be a trashcan or a car coming down the street. They will hear and feel the calmness in your voice and understand the object doesn't mean them any harm. Doing this consistently will actually teach your puppy the names of many objects and increase their vocabulary comprehension.

Praise Your Puppy

People can easily fall into the trap of only talking to their puppy when the puppy is doing something wrong. Praise goes a long way; it isn't always about the food. Our puppies are truly looking for our approval and they really do want our family dynamic to be calm. Make sure you let your puppy know they did a good job and you are happy. Receiving praise as a puppy goes a long way into adulthood.

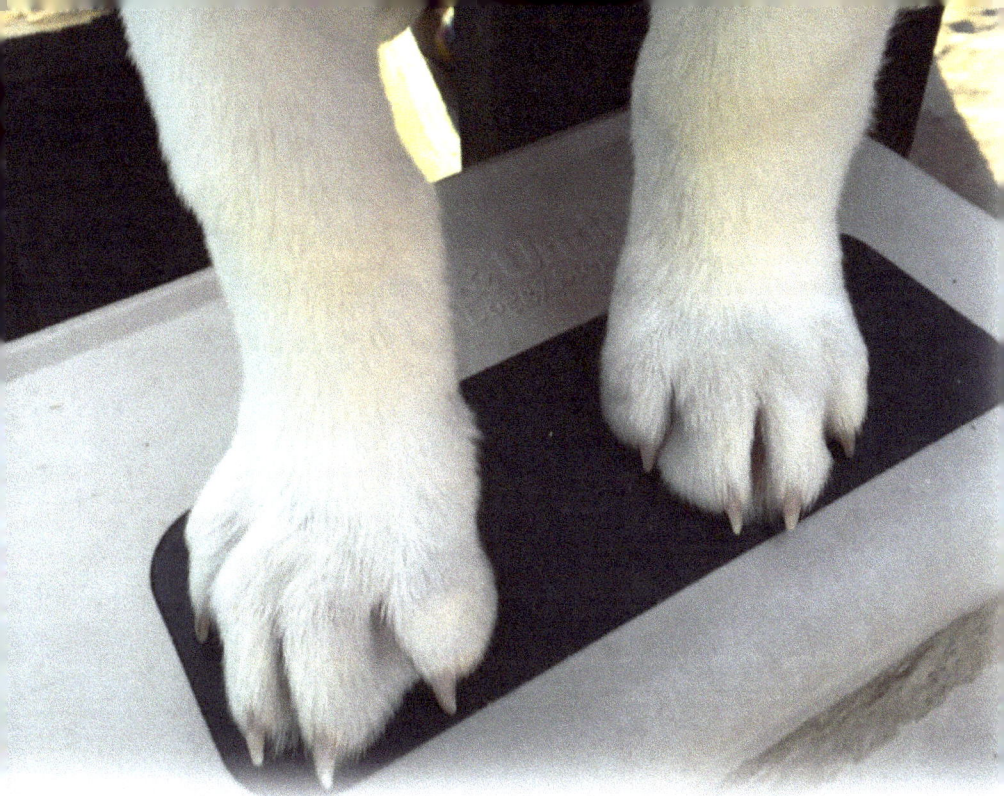

Empowered Puppy Bite #12

Body Awareness

In order to help your puppy be healthy and strong, you need to teach them all about body awareness. You want them to know where their limbs are at all times. You want them to have good coordination and balance, as this helps keep them safe and healthy as an adult. The easiest way to do this is to expose them to various items they can safely climb upon. For example, take a baby pool and fill it with empty water bottles and let them play. This teaches them how to develop their footing on unpredictable surfaces.

Going to the Vet

Think of going to the vet from your puppy's point of view. The environment has such an impact on their perception. You may enter and notice there isn't another dog in sight, but your puppy smells *everything*. They smell the other dogs, they hear the other dogs cry, and, understandably, they are not sure what is going to happen to them. Don't coddle them, but be their advocate. Don't set them on the ground for another dog to come around the corner and scare them. Positive associations from the start will make your puppy love going to the vet.

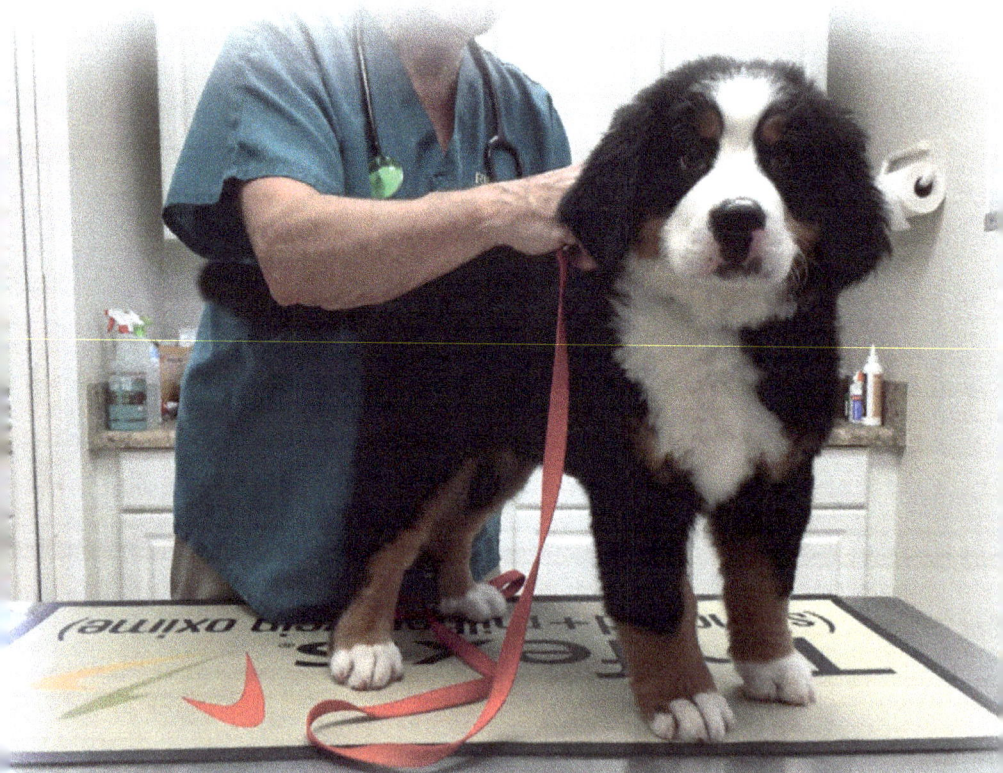

Empowered Puppy Bite #99

Teach Your Puppy to be Alone

At some point you will have to leave your puppy for a time, so they must learn how to be alone. It is best to teach this from the start as habits quickly form, and you don't want the puppy to become reliant upon you always being there. Start with short sessions, when you are still home. Place the puppy in their safe area or crate and go to another area of the home where they can't hear or see you. Gradually build up to longer sessions. The puppy will learn you always come back. This will help ease your mind also, as you know that when you do leave for longer periods of time, they will be fine.

Training Age

The most important time in any puppy's learning abilities is from the age of birth to sixteen weeks of age. Puppies are born with their eyes and ears closed, and so they rely heavily on their amazing sense of smell. Anything you expose to them at this age is quickly absorbed. Even if they do not fully understand a concept or situation, laying a strong foundation at this time, especially in shaping the temperament, will reap years of rewards.

BEHAVIORS

Empowered Puppy Bite #2

Fearful or Aloof

Just like us, puppies can be introverts or extroverts. When you are trying to determine if a puppy is introverted, just being aloof, or is fearful, pay attention to the environment. What is going on around you? Are there lots of distractions? Your puppy's environment plays a huge role in how they interact in any given situation. If they shy away from someone, it may not be the person but the huge truck that just drove by and let out a loud sound.

Empowered Puppy Bite #90

The Raised Paw

The next time you approach a dog, or your puppy approaches another dog, watch the front paws. Raising the paw is a calming signal, so a puppy raising a paw is them being submissive to the other dog. Dogs even do this with people if they feel a bit nervous. It is their way of saying, "I mean you no harm, I just want to be your friend."

Empowered Puppy Bite #83

Stress Signals

Your puppy is always talking to you. Their body language communicates much more than you might imagine. Simple stress signals like licking the lips, the tail being tucked, or not taking a treat will tell you your dog is stressed. There are many things a puppy could be stressed about in any situation, and if you do see signs of stress, the best thing to do is quickly remove them from the environment or trigger that is causing the stress. When you do, you will quickly see them come back to their normal puppy self.

Handling Fear

If you see your puppy in a fearful state, be very careful how you react. Your reaction could actually make that puppy be fearful for their entire life. You have a huge responsibility, as you must teach them in the best way they learn, not how you think they should learn. It is best to remove the puppy from the fearful situation and not coddle them. Talk calmly and do not overexcite them. Avoid saying "it is okay" as that just reinforces the puppy's fears.

Empowered Puppy Bite #43

The Best Time to Train

While your puppy learns constantly, and we encourage training to meet your lifestyle, there are times when you must have a specific training session. Teaching complex behaviors, tricks, cognition games, or concepts requires your puppy to be at their best. Figure out if your puppy is a "morning" puppy or a "nighttime" puppy by noting when they pay attention the best. The easiest way to figure this out is to work with your puppy at three different times during the day. After about three days the best time for your puppy to learn will become clear.

The Clicker. Should I Use It?

As trainers, we think the clicker has a place in dog training, but we do not think it has a place in the hand of an inexperienced user, which many new puppy owners are. Marking a behavior takes precision, know-how, and accurate timing in order for the puppy to know exactly what you expect. Marking good behavior is important in any training program, and a simple marker word such as "yes" is much easier for new puppy owners to say at the right time than clicking the clicker.

Empowered Puppy Bite #92

Scratching is Processing

Sometimes you may ask your puppy to do something, and they just start scratching. You may think that they have an itch, but in fact the puppy is trying to figure out what it is you want. Scratching is something puppies do when they are placed in a situation they are unsure of. Do not keep repeating your command, just give your puppy a few seconds to process what you have asked.

Bite Inhibition

Puppies naturally learn bite inhibition from their littermates between the ages of eight to twelve weeks. So bringing a younger puppy home often leaves the owner's hands and arms free game! They don't realize they are hurting you when they bite. Many people say you should yell a big "OUCH!" to imitate how their littermates scream when the bite hurts, which will make the puppy stop. Well, I am here to tell you firsthand that puppies do not stop; in fact, they bite harder! What you want to do is completely go away from your puppy. When they realize that their biting makes you leave *every* time, guess what . . . the biting stops because they want to keep you near.

Empowered Puppy Bite #81

Sniffing on the Walk

When you are walking your dog or puppy, remember that this is their fun time. We often get so caught up in everyday life, we forget that they are dogs and they like to sniff things. Did you know, their olfactory sense is so strong they can smell their owner from four miles away! So let your puppy be a puppy and enjoy the smells.

Anticipation

Have you ever wondered why, when you ask your puppy to follow a command, such as sit, they immediately follow with lying down? Or maybe you ask for one paw and they give you both. Your puppy has learned to anticipate what you are asking because you have become predictable. So mix things up! Try to be as random as you can, and it will actually strengthen your puppy's behaviors.

Empowered Puppy Bite #97

Fear Period

One of the most fearful times of a puppy's life is when they are between eight and eleven weeks of age. That is also often the time that they leave the breeder. You need to be conscious of this and careful not to reinforce fears during this stage. If you see that your puppy is nervous about something, react calmly. Guide them through their nervousness by explaining the situation. Make sure you do not coddle them as that will reinforce the fear, which could come back to haunt you when they turn eight or nine months old and go through their teenage fear period.

Can I Play with That?

When your puppy is little it is important to pay attention to what they are playing with. Sometimes, what they do when they are little is cute and doesn't do too much damage. But keep in mind, if you let them chew on your shoes when they are younger, they are going to chew on them when they get older. They will not understand if they are not allowed to chew or play with the same things they did when they were little.

Empowered Puppy Bite #95

Bad Behavior

The number one cause of bad behavior in a puppy or a dog is boredom. Often the smartest puppies are the most destructive. It is very much like the child who enters kindergarten but really should be in third grade. With a puppy, make sure you pay just as much attention to their mental well-being as you do their physical well-being. Puppies get much more tired with mental stimulation, so get them thinking. Hide some kibble under your hand and teach them to find it. Teach them to ring a call bell. Teach them to imitate you and your actions. All these will make for a well-rounded puppy who is less likely to look for trouble.

Empowered Puppy Bite #9

Tale of the Tails

The best way to determine your dog's mood is by looking at the tail. It will tell you how they feel. But if it is wagging, don't always assume that means they are happy to see you. It could mean they are happy to eat you! If the tail is straight down, they are feeling very cautious, while straight up in the air means they are highly aroused and alert. A tail tucked between the legs means they are nervous about a situation. As you train your puppy, pay attention to the tail. If it suddenly changes from happy to aroused or cautious, take note of your environment to determine what could be distracting them.

Empowered Puppy Bite #39

Good and Bad Behaviors

Many of your puppy's behaviors that you might deem as bad are actually good behaviors to them. Barking, digging, or chewing are natural behaviors to them. For us, not so much. Barking? Put it on command. Digging? Give them an area where they are allowed to dig. Chewing? Show them what they are allowed to chew. Using adverse methods to change a puppy's natural instincts is, in our opinion, the worst way to handle it.

Scent Associations

Remember when your grandma baked cookies and the house was filled with that familiar heavenly smell? Then years later you could be somewhere and get a whiff of cookies baking and your memory whisks you back to the days of Grandma's baking. Your dog has the same capabilities but even more so, as they associate specific scents with actions, events, places, and people. Often, we assume it is a sound or person making our dog nervous, when it is actually a smell. Maybe your dog goes crazy at the sound of thunder, but really it is the smell of the rain.

Empowered Puppy Bite #105

Wagging Tails

When you see a dog wagging its tail a hundred miles a minute and wiggling its little butt all over the place, you assume the dog is happy to see you. But do you really know what that tail wagging means? Research has determined that if a dog wags its tail in a complete circle, it is hugely excited to see you. If the tail wags to the dog's right, then the dog is happy to see you but not gushing with excitement. If the tail wags to the left of the dog's body, they are unsure of you, so proceed with caution. The next time you greet a dog, take note of the direction of the tail wag to understand how the dog is feeling.

Greeting New People

Greeting new people can be hard for the puppy and hard for you. New people see your cute little puppy and let them jump up, something we don't want to teach. Some people are a little "too much" and your puppy may make the wrong association with strangers. Teach your puppy to have manners and sit before anyone can pet them.

Empowered Puppy Bite #3

Carry Something for Anxious Barking

If you have determined that your dog is barking because of fear or anxiety, give them something to hold in their mouth. A stuffed animal to clamp down on helps them curb anxiety. If they get anxious on a walk or going to the vet, let them take the toy along. It's a release for them and a coping mechanism that will help them deal with the situation and not bark.

Chewing

Many people turn to the sprays available for purchase to deter their puppy's chewing. We don't think you should use them, and here's why: They tend to be made with various chemicals that your puppy doesn't need. Puppies don't know the difference between a table leg or a bone. They don't know that is your good dining room chair; they're just looking for something to chomp down on. So, from the start, make sure to have plenty of things your puppy can chew safely on. If they go for something they shouldn't be chewing, just redirect to something acceptable.

Empowered Puppy Bite #78

Counter Surfers

Counter surfing is an issue some people have with their dogs. What happens is that when the puppy is little, you stand by your counter, often preparing food, and the puppy jumps up at you for attention. Oftentimes, you will push them down, then reward them with a treat from the counter for listening. Well, they are so smart they just learned that things on the counter taste good, and they want them! The easiest way to change this behavior is to walk away from the counter and ask your dog to sit or lie and wait. Reward them away from the counter so they learn the reward is coming from you, not the counter.

OBEDIENCE

Empowered Puppy Bite #44

How Long to Train

Training times for your new puppy should be short and sweet. The best way to make sure a puppy learns in various ways is to train throughout your day. Whether you ask them to sit and wait while you do the dishes, or they are lying by your side while you work on the computer, training during your daily life gets them used to what you expect. You get your work done and they get trained at the same time.

Motivation Food or Toy

Mix things up for your puppy. Don't always reward with food. Toys make a great reward as well. You can even reward with a food-stuffed toy so they learn how to interact with the toy and the food. Also, don't forget to add praise as a reward; if you are in a place where you cannot reward with a toy or food, reward with your approval and a fake air treat. We sometimes will act as if we are giving a treat even though we don't have one. The puppies will smell, swallow, and sometimes chew something that isn't even there!

Empowered Puppy Bite #22

Don't Rush the Walk

Many people collect their puppy and immediately want to go for a walk around the neighborhood to show the puppy off. Our advice is, don't rush to go on the walk! Leash pulling is a problem that many dogs face because as puppies they were allowed to pull on the leash from the day they came home. Walk your dog in your yard, with the leash dragging at first. Then after a few days pick up the leash and continue in your yard. Once the puppy is not pulling and is focusing on you, then you can venture out into the neighborhood. They must be taught leash manners in a non-distracting area first, before you can hit the road.

Why Wait?

We teach "wait" instead of "stay" as it helps in many other areas of training. With waiting, we "count" in order to keep the puppy's mind occupied. This prevents dopamine levels rising in their brain. So, if a siren goes off, we can say "wait" and count until the siren stops. The puppy learns "wait" is a temporary time element, and they learn to be more reliable. We can also ask them to go into their crate and "wait." Once again, they learn the temporary element that helps them understand and process better.

Empowered Puppy Bite #6

Teaching a Puppy to Wait

When teaching your puppy to wait, do it in three parts. To begin, ask for a duration wait, where you may count to ten. Then add some movement and reward the puppy for waiting in position. The third part is walking away. Don't walk away facing your puppy; simply turn your back and very quickly go a few short steps. Come back to reward them. If you start training your puppy by backing up with your hand out and repeating the command over and over, that puppy will break the wait every time you turn your back.

Here or Come

Whether you use the command "here" or "come," start teaching your puppy when you are inside. You need to make sure they fully understand the command before entering the distracting world outside. Call your puppy and have them automatically sit when they arrive. Always reward with a treat for coming, as you want the puppy to associate the command with getting a treat every time. If you don't have a treat on you, use an "air treat." This is when you simply act like you are giving a treat, and the puppy will eagerly take it and may even chew the air!

Empowered Puppy Bite #31

Here With a Target

Many puppies, when called to "come" or "here," will associate it with their owner leaving. You call the puppy, the puppy comes, then they go in the crate. So they will often ignore the command just to get a few more minutes with their owner. This obviously isn't ideal if we are running late for work. At Training Canines, we teach our puppies to "here" instead of "come." We offer this as a complex behavior in order for the puppy not to make any associations. We use a two-finger target. We call the puppy and they are to touch their nose to our two fingers, then automatically sit. We then reward them, which to them ends the behavior and they won't make the association with us leaving.

End on a Positive Note

As you work with your puppy you will see that they learn very quickly. It's easy to get excited by this and want to see what else you can teach them. Don't get greedy for success, as you always want to end even a simple session on a positive note. This will make them eager to work with you again, and oftentimes they will try even harder as they have learned how they made you happy previously.

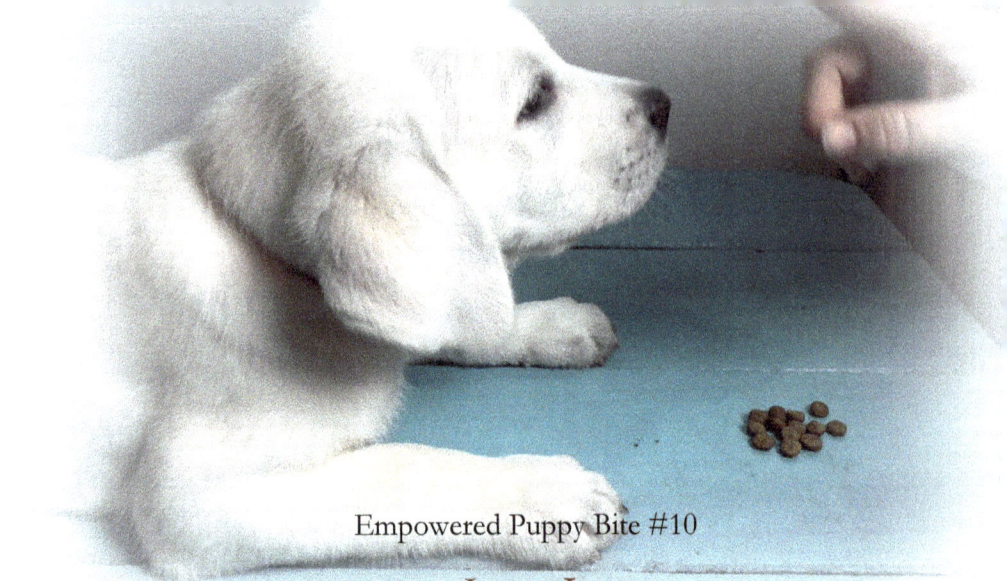

Empowered Puppy Bite #10

Leave It

"Leave it" is a command you want your puppy to learn from the start. It means they are never to have the item in their mouth. So "leave it" works for everything from rocks to socks to puppy biting on your arm. Simply start by holding a piece of kibble in one hand as the reward. Place another piece of kibble down in front of your puppy and cover it with your hand. They will try like crazy to get it. You say "leave it" and be ready, because the second they look away from the covered kibble, reward them with the kibble from the opposite hand. You will be surprised how quickly they learn this. However, when they are younger they forget quickly and the next time you do it, they might act as if they never have learned it. But don't get discouraged. It just takes a few weeks of consistency, and it is amazing how strong this command becomes.

62

Hand Signals

As you teach your puppy their commands, be careful that you do not incorporate hand signals. Many will say "sit" to their puppy at the same time as making a hand gesture. The puppy will follow the hand gesture long before they learn the word. Why does that matter? Well, what if your puppy is running away from you and you need to have them sit to avoid danger? They can't see your hand but they will definitely hear the word "sit"!

Empowered Puppy Bite #7

Jumping

Many people inadvertently teach their puppies to jump up from the day they get them. Imagine it: This adorable puppy comes running to you and you go ahead and push them down or perhaps pet them. All of this is a reward to the puppy! The best thing to do is stand up or move away without even making eye contact with the puppy. Ask them to sit, and if they do, reward them with your attention. If they jump up again, you stand up and look away. You will be amazed just how quickly they get it.

Watch

You can't teach your dog anything if you don't have their attention or focus. When you say the puppy's name, wait until they look at you, and put it on command by saying "watch." You can also point to your eyes so your puppy will learn they must make eye contact with you.

Empowered Puppy Bite #26

The Word No

If you choose to use the word no with your puppy, avoid associating it with the puppy's name. You want to keep the name positive so when you say it they quickly respond to you. Tagging their name with no has the same negative effect on them as it would if someone kept associating your name with no. Instead, use "no ma'am" or "no sir," or give the puppy a little "eh eh," to let them know they are not acting appropriately.

Top Three Ways Your Puppy Can Learn Faster

1: Play with the puppy before and after you train.

2: Keep your sessions short.

3: Let the puppy take a little nap and they will retain more of what you taught them.

Empowered Puppy Bite #53

Waiting at the Door

Nobody wants to open the door and have the puppy rush out or jump on the person on the other side. First, work with your puppy by having them sit prior to you opening the door. If they get up, the door shuts. If they stay sitting, the door opens. Work slowly with asking them to wait. Take baby steps and progress a little at a time, ending with your puppy being able to wait with the door open while you walk outside and come back inside. If your puppy gets excited and pushes forward, just go back to the step where they were able to contain themselves. Have short, consistent sessions, and never push too hard.

Off-Leash Walking

One of the things we teach here at Training Canines is walking off leash. We teach the puppy to want to stay with us. We want them to have the freedom to explore, yet we want them to be aware of where we are. We want to give them the impression it is their responsibility to keep track of us, not us of them (even though we are watching that they are safe every second). This is how you can do the same: Place the puppy on a leash and let them drag the leash. Walking back and forth in a safe area, let them wander. When they come back to you, reward with praise and a treat. If you are going to continue training your dog to be off leash in different places, please remember safety first. Take note of where you are, making sure there are no cars and no way your dog can get hurt. You never know if they will see something to chase, so always keep the leash on as it is easier to grab a leash than a collar.

Empowered Puppy Bite #27

Training the Opposites

One of the easiest ways for your puppy to understand what you would like them to do is to teach them in opposites. They must know the feeling of calmness in order to know how to react when you tell them to settle down. They must know the feeling of being alert when you need them to be on guard. So, when you see your puppy is calm or alert, just put the feeling on command by naming it, just as you would any other command such as *sit*.

Like Me

Our research uncovered that we could actually teach puppies through imitation as early as four weeks old. We teach them the concept of copying our actions. Whether it be something simple such as ringing a bell, or more complicated like performing a sequence, some puppies really enjoy this learning style. But be warned: This can backfire! We actually taught a puppy to jump the fence because we stepped over it all the time. They are constantly watching you, so be careful what you teach!

Empowered Puppy Bite #62

Sitting Anywhere

Here is a fun training game to play with your puppy that helps them learn to generalize: the sitting game. Does your dog know how to sit if you ask when you are sitting? Do they know how to sit if you are instructing from another room? How about when you are lying down, or facing the opposite direction? Practice in different places and positions to make sure your dog truly knows how to sit. You will be surprised at how much they really do know.

Waiting in the Line of Sight

When you begin teaching your puppy to stay or wait, always do so in their line of sight. If you walk behind a puppy or go at an angle where they have to turn their body to see you, nine times out of ten they will break the wait. Set them up for success at all times.

Empowered Puppy Bite #61

Proficiency

How will you know if your puppy fully understands what you
are teaching? Well, if they can perform the task eight out of ten
trials, you can say they are proficient with that task. Just take it
slow, and they will retain more.

CRATE TRAINING

Crate Size

There's a common practice of placing a puppy in a big crate from the start, saying they will grow into it. It's best to avoid this, because if a puppy is placed in too large a crate, they will use one side for the bathroom and the other side to sleep. Make sure it's big enough that they can turn around comfortably and stand. Also, be careful if you place them in the crate with a collar on. It can easily get caught on the crate. Some people place blankets or boxes inside the crate to make it smaller, which is fine, as long as whatever you put inside cannot be eaten or be a choking hazard.

Crate Training

You will find many tips on crate training, and, in our opinion, one of the main tips to remember is to look at it from your puppy's perspective. The puppy has been with their mom and littermates for the first eight weeks or more of their life. While you are excited to take them home, they have no clue what just happened. Put the puppy in your room at least for the first few nights, or longer if needed. If they begin to cry in the night, see if they need to eliminate. Do not talk with them, as you do not want to overstimulate them so they can't go back to sleep. If they are crying and you know they don't have to go potty, simply let them smell you. If you think they have to go, just carry the puppy outside to go and bring them right back in. You may need to lie on the floor by the crate just so they know you are there. Avoid eye contact as a puppy will take that and run with it! Just let them smell your hand. It will get better after just a few days.

Day and Nighttime Crate Training

It helps significantly to teach your puppy how to act in their crate during the day and at night. Having two different crates will also help. You can teach them that they can go in their crate with a bone or toy while you are around the home. This prepares them for when you finally leave them, as they have become used to being in the crate. For nighttime, keep the crate close to where you sleep. Your scent of being there with everything quiet and calm will be consoling. Avoid talking with them at night as that can be overstimulating. You can even play soft music in order to help them settle down if they are a bit whiny.

Empowered Puppy Bite #72

Sleeping Through the Night

Sleeping through the night is something every puppy owner looks forward to. Some puppies manage it earlier than others of the same age, however there is a big difference in maturity between a ten-week-old puppy and a thirteen-week-old puppy. At ten weeks, puppies are usually getting up twice a night. At thirteen weeks, the puppy usually can go down around 11 p.m. and make it until 3 or 4 a.m. By the time they hit fifteen weeks they should be sleeping all the way through the night.

How Long to Stay in the Crate?

The general rule is: your puppy's age plus one hour. Therefore, a puppy that is two months old should be able to spend up to three hours in a crate, and so on. There are many variables to that, though, such as how much water they have had, time of day, whether they were playful when you put them in the crate, when was the last time they went to the bathroom, and so on. Make note of all the factors when you're calculating the time, rather than following general rules.

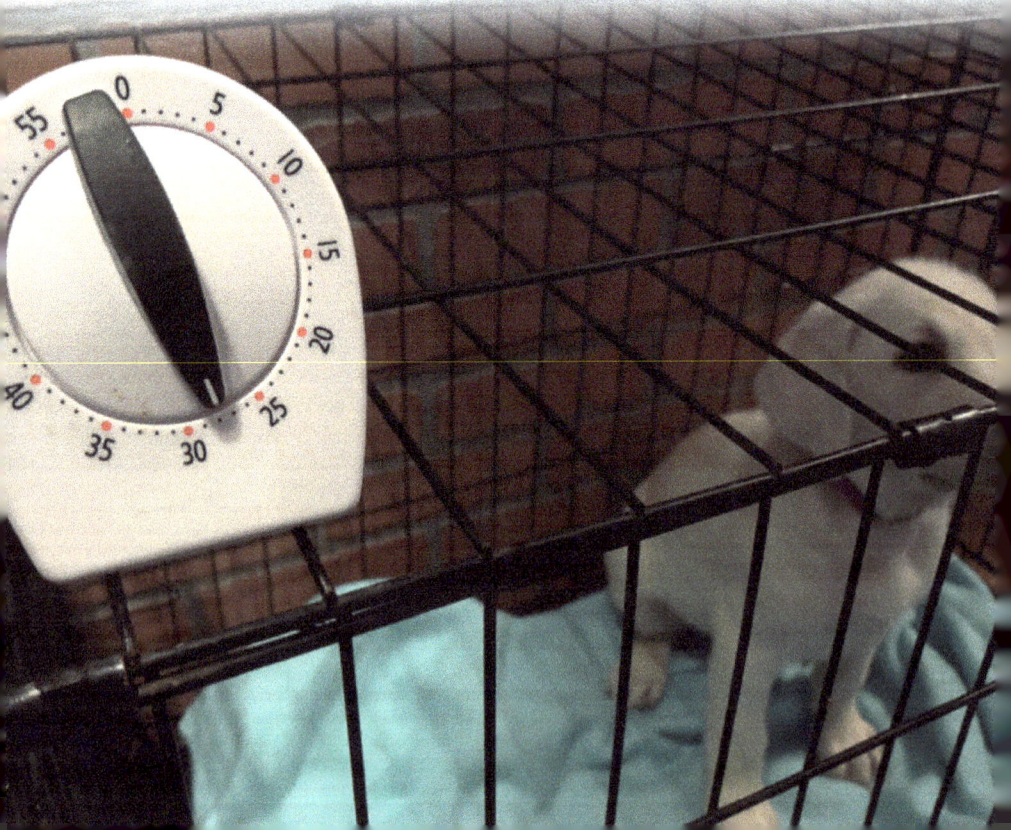

POTTY TRAINING

The Number One Reason Potty Training Fails

The number one reason people fail in housetraining their puppy is because they give the puppy too much freedom from the start. The feeling of needing to eliminate comes upon them very quickly; puppies under eight weeks of age have no bladder or bowel control at all. Your puppy's space needs to be limited when they are younger. If they have a distance to go to the door, they will have an accident. Keep them in close range of the area where you want them to eliminate.

Empowered Puppy Bite #58

Potty Accidents

If you catch your puppy in the act of going to the bathroom in the house, do not yell. You do not want to scare them, because if you do scare them, they will quickly learn to hide going to the bathroom if you are near. What you should do instead is calmly walk up to them and say "no ma'am" or "no sir" pick them up, and say, "let's go potty outside" and take them outside to the appropriate area. Make sure to reward or acknowledge they are doing it correctly.

First Potty of the Day

When potty training your new puppy, make sure that first thing in the morning, you carry them from the crate to the designated potty spot. If you give them the opportunity to walk to the door, more than likely they will have an accident on the way. By carrying the puppy, you can be sure that they will eliminate in the appropriate area, and you can reward and praise them for doing such a great job.

Potty Time or Play Time

A problem we often hear from new puppy owners is that they take their puppy out to go potty, the puppy doesn't go, and upon returning to the house the puppy goes on the floor. This is simple to prevent: Start from the day you bring the puppy home. Use two doors if you can—one to go to the potty area, and one to go play. You want to make a simple association that you are out so the puppy can eliminate, and that is it. No playing. Many owners let their dogs play as they wait for them to go, but this is a mistake. Stand with your puppy so you can say "great job." As soon as they finish, take them back in. Give them a few seconds, then go out the second door and name it "playtime" or whatever you wish. So now you have a "potty time" door and a "playtime" door.

Potty On and Off the Leash

We have learned that you must train a puppy to relieve themselves both on and off the leash. Puppies have a hard time generalizing, so we need to make it as simple and clear as we can. Sometimes they can go outside to eliminate on a leash, sometimes freestyle. This way, if you need them to go potty on a walk they can do it, or if you need them to go in the open yard free of a leash, they can do that too.

SOCIALIZATION

Starting Socialization

Socialization is crucial for any puppy's development and beyond. It's best to start as soon as your puppy comes home, but do so safely. Avoid pet stores, as your puppy is not yet fully protected and could pick up a parasite or virus. Take them places in a shopping buggy that you can place a towel inside, and don't let them get nose-to-nose with dogs you don't know. Even if an older dog appears healthy, it can carry a virus that a younger puppy could pick up. Safety is paramount during any socialization trip.

Empowered Puppy Bite #5

Don't Feed Fear

When you take your brand-new puppy out in public, you may begin to see behaviors like jumping up, hiding behind you, or even a bit of whining. These are all ways a puppy processes fears. It is important to let them work through this themselves. Avoid pushing people, situations, or other dogs on them, as that will make them more insecure. Do not say the usual "it's okay" because that will only reinforce their fear. Just go slowly and let them process it on their own.

Different Surfaces

Teaching your puppy about different textures on the ground is an important part of socialization. They need to walk on as many surfaces as they can—grass, mulch, pine needles, even stones. All of these surfaces create different sensations on your puppy's feet. They also need to learn about surfaces in the house, such as hardwood floors, carpet, and tile. If they are not exposed to these different surfaces in their younger days, they may become fearful of them as they get older.

Empowered Puppy Bite #51

Meeting Other Dogs

When you bring a new puppy home they are going to be very excited when meeting new dogs. Whether it be your existing dog or one you meet on the street, you need to take control of the situation in order for your puppy not to be too boisterous or fearful. When dogs greet each other, they sniff the other dog's rear end. That is their handshake and introduction. The simplest and easiest way to have your puppy meet a new dog is to let both dogs do just that. Hold your puppy in your arms and let the other dog sniff your puppy's behind, then let your puppy do the same. Set the puppy down and just monitor their interactions.

Car Riding

Picking up a new puppy is very exciting for you, but not so much for the puppy. While safety in the car is of utmost concern, the puppy's mental state is also important. Our advice on how to handle that first car ride is this: Do not take a crate, place it in the back of your car, put the puppy in, and head off. This would create a negative association with the crate. If you are going to use a crate, you need to be able to sit right next to it as you will want to give the puppy the comfort of someone being by their side. If it is going to be a longer drive and you will need to feed your puppy on the way, feed small amounts from your hand. This will help their stomach settle if they are feeling nervous. Do not give all the food at once as it potentially could cause car sickness. If you have to stop for them to eliminate, do so in a place where other dogs are limited. Avoid the rest areas, as your puppy is not yet fully protected and could pick up a parasite.

FOOD. FEEDING. TREATS

The Food Obsession

One thing you should remember about puppies (especially Labrador Retrievers), is they will eat and eat and eat. A puppy needs almost three times the amount of food as they will when they are an adult. If you don't want your puppy turning into an overweight adult (and obviously you don't), take precautions when they are young. Weigh the food instead of using a scoop or cup measure. Using a scale to portion the food will ensure they are eating the proper amount.

Empowered Puppy Bite #57

Table Food

Is table food okay for your dog? Well, that depends on what is
on your table! Think about what you are eating. Is it healthy? Is
it whole food or is it processed? If you know that what you are
eating is good for you and safe for them, then sure, table food is
fine. But also think about where you are giving the food. If you
don't want your puppy to constantly be waiting at the table, you
might want to go into a different room before feeding them a
little treat from your plate.

Food Guarding

We want to teach the puppy that they have to wait and that we control the food source. This helps prevent resource guarding of their food. We sit close by while they eat, and place our hands by the bowl, pick up the bowl, even take the bowl and walk away. Make the puppy sit and then let them have it back. Make them wait for you to set the bowl back down, as this will help with self-control and the puppy will learn you are the keeper of all good things.

Empowered Puppy Bite #104

Water

Did you ever consider your dog or puppy's water source? There are many different sources we can provide our dog: bottled water, tap water, distilled drinking water, and more. Some researchers say dogs can taste water; dogs have 1,700 taste buds (compared with a human's 9,000), located at the tip of the tongue. Water treated with fluoride is not good for dogs. The best water to give them is filtered water right from the tap, not bottled water. So there's no need to spend extra money.

Feeding Times

How much and how many times a day to feed a puppy can be confusing. Different manufacturers and well-meaning friends tend to give different instructions. We feed three to four meals spaced out throughout the day, and always at the same time. If you feed a puppy at a given time, their bathroom habits will become routine. Feeding several times a day keeps them satisfied and is better for their digestion. It is just like the advice given for people: more meals but smaller. Puppies are the same.

Empowered Puppy Bite #56

Changing the Feeding Routine

When feeding your puppy, it is important to expose them to many different containers and places. Vary it by using a paper plate or ceramic bowl. Feed them inside or outside, on the carpet or on the wooden floor. Feeding them in all areas and in different dishes will teach them to generalize feeding time, and they won't refuse to eat if you change the routine.

Differentiate Your Treats

Would you work for free? Neither will your puppy. In order for a puppy to learn what you are teaching, there has to be a positive reward. It is best to reward with a small food treat, like kibble, and praise. In the beginning you will reward everything they do. As they learn, your food rewards will lessen, although the praise must *always* be there. As they grow they will want to explore more, and they will become more distracted, so you can change to higher-value treats to keep their attention.

Empowered Puppy Bite #107

Rawhide Treats

This is important, so please take it to heart: *Never, ever* give your puppy or dog rawhide treats. Rawhide is not only a huge choking hazard, it can also cause severe gastrointestinal blockages. Rawhide is a byproduct of the leather-making process and is chemically treated with all kinds of preservatives and artificial colors. We can't stress this enough: **Never give rawhide treats to your puppy or dog.**

GENERAL PUPPY CARE

Empowered Puppy Bite #38

Puppy Classes

With good intentions, many new puppy owners rush right into puppy classes at the local big box stores. We are all for people training their new puppy and being responsible; however, you need to make sure your puppy is ready. Puppies learn 24/7, whether what they are learning is good or bad. Teaching core behaviors to a new puppy in a calm environment devoid of distractions is crucial. Oftentimes, group classes are a bit chaotic with lots of puppies and people. Some puppies do great, and others not so much. Puppies learn from imitation, so they easily could learn to run around crazily like the cute puppy across the room. Don't rush to the classes without knowing your puppy's learning skills. Work with the puppy at home. If you want to take them at a later date to socialize, that is great. But start the day you bring your puppy home, in your own home, and build their confidence before you rush out to that class.

What Colors Should Toys Be?

Your puppy is not capable of seeing the color red, yet if you go into your local pet store you'll see that the majority of the toys are red. Wonder why? Red is an impact color and they want you, the puppy owner, to buy the toy. Dogs see shades of blue, green, brown, and gray. That red ball sitting on your green grass looks almost black to your puppy. So, get toys they can see, and think of contrast when you do. A blue or yellow ball would be a better choice than green if they will be playing with the ball on a grassy field.

Empowered Puppy Bite #15

Name Recognition

A mistake many people make is repeating a command over and over when the puppy is not even looking at them. Next time you ask your puppy to do something, say their name first. This will pull their focus and attention to you and then you can tell them what you would like them to do.

Myth: Dogs Automatically Know How to Swim

Many people believe, as we did years ago, that all dogs know how to swim. But this is not the case. Swimming is a learned behavior. Don't force your puppy into the water. Take it slow and encourage them to go at the pace their temperament and personality can handle. *Never* just throw your dog or puppy into the water as that only creates a risk of injury and a bad association with water.

Empowered Puppy Bite #84

The Right Way to Pet a Puppy

Under the chin! This is the most comfortable way for you to pet a puppy or any dog. Oftentimes, if you reach to pet the top of their head, they will flinch as their eyes don't catch your hand approaching until it is very close. Dogs see differently than we do; when we are looking straight at a dog's face, they do not see the center of our face, only two eyes looking back at them. They are able to see us better if we stand slightly to the side so that we are looking at an angle to the puppy or dog.

Everyone Needs to Train

Every member of the family must take part in training your new puppy. You want the puppy to bond with everyone, not just one person. If you have children, include them. Make sure that you work with them and the puppy together, so the children understand how to teach the puppy. Have the other person or child hold a treat in the palm of their hand and have the puppy take it. This will instantly create a positive association between them. Build the relationships slowly and earn trust.

Empowered Puppy Bite #87

The Retractable Leash

At Training Canines, we feel retractable leashes are a big no-no. Think about how a retractable leash works. Your puppy has to pull on it for the leash to extend. It is very easy to forget to lock it into place at a certain length, and they could get hurt. On a walk, you don't have any control over what may shoot out in front of you that your puppy will want to chase. Another dog could approach and the line could tangle. Or, even worse, a car may go by and your puppy is too far away from you to have any control. All in all, you are better off with a standard five-foot leash so you know the puppy is by your side.

Puppy Daycare

Doggy daycare is another area where you need to be sure of the puppy's surroundings. If one puppy is doing it, usually they are all doing it. Structured daycare is great if it is operated by people who know what to look for in puppy play. Often, signals are missed, and your puppy could wind up learning some not-so-great stuff. While you think they are coming home tired from having had a great time, they could have just been totally stressed from hiding from the other puppies.

Empowered Puppy Bite #52

Realistic Expectations

Many people have the attitude that their puppy must obey them all the time and pay attention to every word they say. Being a puppy is tough, as everything is new. They are constantly learning about all the things in your world. One day they will be spot on and do everything you ask. The next day they will give you a look of despair and not know what to do. This is all part of maturing and learning. It is the puppy trying to figure it out, and your job is to provide guidance and support.

Bath Time

Your puppy's first bath doesn't have to be stressful or frustrating for you or your puppy. Just like trimming their nails or cleaning their ears, you want to take it slow and easy. One way you can do that is to let the puppy hang out in a very shallow bath to get used to the water. The water should be warm. Use a bowl and slowly pour the water over their body, talking with them the entire time. Tell them what is happening. Don't just grab the hose and try to wash them like you wash the car.

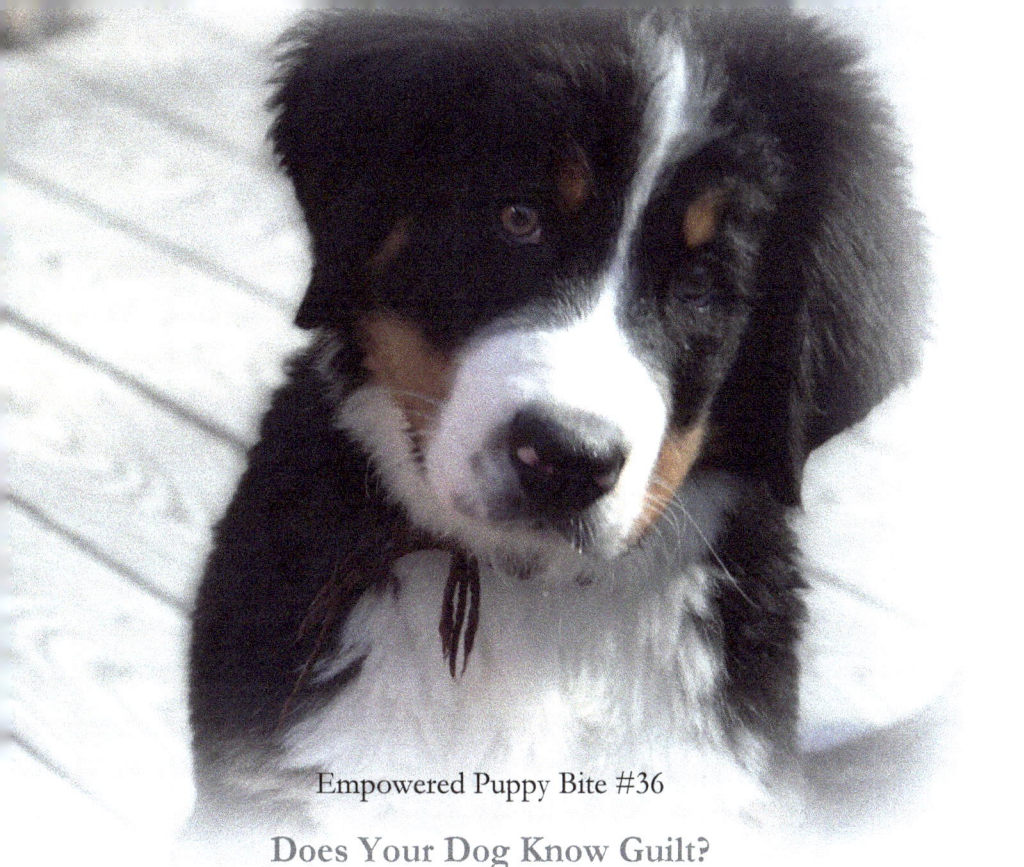

Empowered Puppy Bite #36

Does Your Dog Know Guilt?

You come in and the newspaper is torn to pieces and you ask your dog if they did that. They sink down and give you a look that you might swear is a guilty look, and there you go—full admission. Well, not really. What actually happens is that you walk in the door and see things are not normal and your anxiety level changes. This changes your scent because your perspiration changes. Your dog's olfactory skills go to work and detect this immediately. They begin to worry about what is wrong and will give you that look, which is actually just a reaction to your reaction!

Motion Sickness

It is not uncommon for a puppy to get motion sickness during a car ride. They might drool excessively, pant, or even vomit. One option to help them get used to the motion is to work with them in a pool or even a bathtub or large sink. Take a child's boogie board or foam kickboard and place the puppy on it in very shallow water. If you are using a pool, please make sure the puppy has a life jacket and is fully protected if they fall in. Have them sit or stand or whatever is comfortable for them. Make sure they do not get water in the ears, eyes, or nose. In fact, they should not touch the water at all. Hold the puppy and carefully rock the board slightly to create an unstable feeling. As they get comfortable, you can increase the motion.

Empowered Puppy Bite #109

Puppy Barking

Sometimes a puppy will start barking and you just don't know why. Puppies bark for attention, for fun, because they are bored, and out of fear. If you are sure your puppy is not fearful and seems to be barking for one of the other reasons, turn it into a game. Put the barking on command. Teach them to bark and teach them to be quiet. By teaching them the opposites, it becomes very easy for them to understand and learn what you are asking.

Patience and Humor

Often our days are pretty stressful, and we feel the frustration of everything weighing on us. When we are anxious or upset, our bodies produce a scent-specific perspiration that our dogs pick up immediately. Some dogs begin to go into a console mode while others become anxious themselves. Your puppy will feed off your emotion. If you need to, take a deep breath and let whatever is bothering roll off your back. Laugh or go look in the mirror and smile. Keeping things in perspective will teach you to have patience and humor as you teach your puppy.

BEHAVIORS

CRATE TRAINING

FOOD. FEEDING. TREATS

GENERAL PUPPY CARE

OBEDIENCE

POTTY TRAINING

SOCIALIZATION

TEMPERAMENT

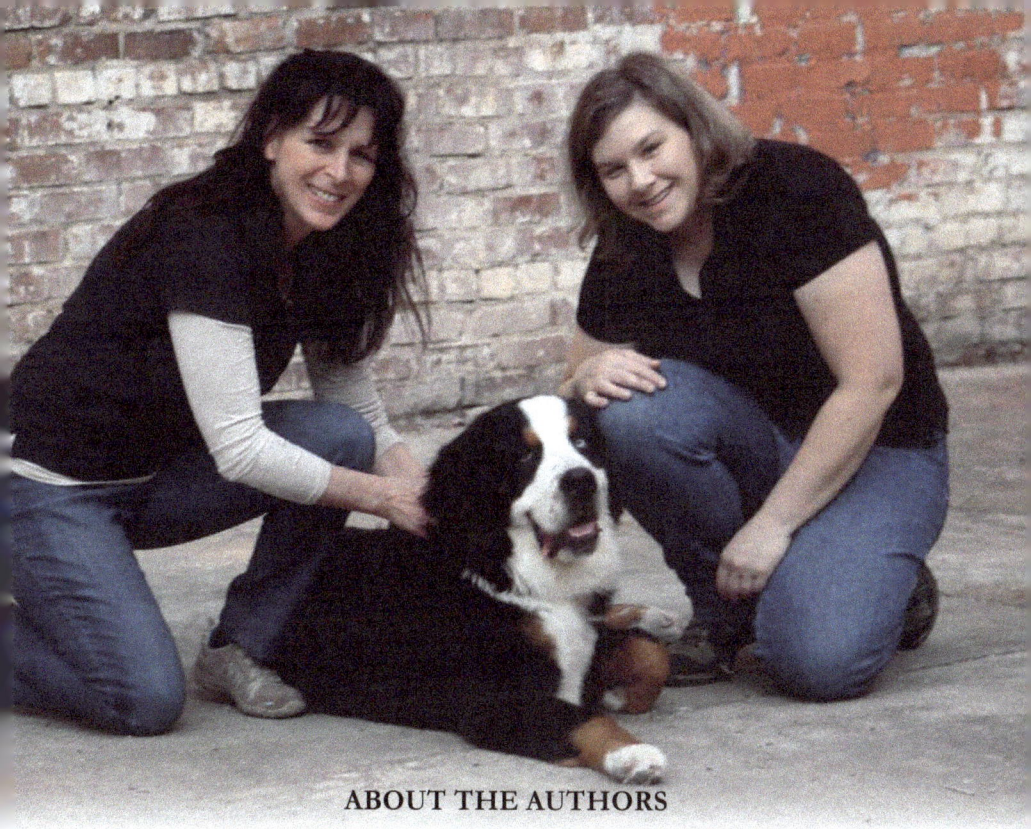

ABOUT THE AUTHORS

Kim Paciotti CPDT-KA, founder of Training Canines, LLC specializes in early puppy development. Kim is a certified trainer with the Council of Certified Professional Dog Trainers (CCPDT) and many refer to her as a Canine Scientist, and Puppy Specialist. Kim is also a Professional Member of the Association of Pet Dog Trainers (APDT). She is a graduate of Highland Canine Training in both on- and off-leash obedience. Kim continued her education at Animal Behavior College for training rescue and shelter dogs. She completed the Dog Cognition & Emotion course offered by Brian Hare at Duke University. Being an AKC Canine Good Citizen Evaluator, she knows what is expected to pass this test. Kim is an approved evaluator for the National Therapy Dog Registry.

Her research within the field of puppy training led Kim to create The Empowered Puppy Program, an exciting approach to training the whole puppy—mentally, physically, and socially. Kim believes that solving the ongoing issue of dog surrenders to shelters and rescues begins with a solid foundation in puppyhood. Kim's research has proven over and over that training puppies from an early age, and to their individual personalities, stops unwanted behaviors before they begin and builds a strong relationship between dog and owner. It is her desire to change the way people understand and 'do' training by teaching them that it's about working with your lifestyle and your puppy, not against them. Kim is passionate about changing the world one puppy at a time!

Kim lives in Statesville, NC with her husband David, and her two English Mastiffs Sammy and Bernard.

Christina Borders lives in North Carolina on a small farm with her two dogs, Pheobe and Beignet, and a menagerie of other animals. Working with dogs has always been a touchstone in her life and has grown into an amazing adventure with Kim and the puppies of Training Canines. She is passionate about exploring the possibilities of the canine mind while working to promote and deepen the human-dog bond through education.

She enjoys learning and analyzing new ways to approach training and relating to the dogs who share our lives. They motivate her to keep moving forward, always looking for the next discovery or lightbulb moment.

In her free time Christina enjoys photographing animals and nature, as well as sculpting.

Contact Information:

Foundational Trained Puppies for Assistance-Therapy-Pets
http://www.trainingcanines.com
Training for Breeders and Trainers
http://www.empoweredpuppy.com
Online Puppy School for New Puppy Owners
http://www.empoweredpuppyschool.com
Healthy Eats with Dr. Cos and Empowered Pups Fan Page
http://www.empoweredpups.com

Facebook:
https://www.facebook.com/trainingcanines
Twitter:
@empoweredpuppy
Youtube:
https://www.youtube.com/empoweredpups
Instagram:
https://www.instagram.com/empoweredpuppyprogram/
Pinterest:
https://www.pinterest.com/empoweredpuppy/

www.ingramcontent.com/pod-product-compliance
Lightning Source LLC
Chambersburg PA
CBHW041823090426
42811CB00010B/1091